STUDIO PRESS

First published in the UK in 2018 by Studio Press,
an imprint of Kings Road Publishing, part of Bonnier Publishing,
The Plaza, 535 King's Road, London, SW10 0SZ
www.studiopressbooks.co.uk
www.bonnierpublishing.com

© 2018 Studio Press

1 3 5 7 9 10 8 6 4 2
0410718

All rights reserved
ISBN 978-1-78741-4600

Written by Laura Baker
Edited by Matt Yeo
Designed by Jeannette O'Toole
for Cloud King Creative

Printed in the United Kingdom

PAINTING ROCKS

Join the hide-and-find craze!

Contents

Welcome to the Wonderful World of Painting Rocks!	6
Getting Started	8
Tips and Tricks	10
Cute Creatures	12
Words of Wisdom	16
Inspiring Images	20
Cool Colours	24
Pretty Patterns	28
Fun Food	32
Black and White	36

Location, Location	40
Little Monsters	44
Shaped Rocks	48
Art Templates	52
Words of Wisdom	56
Hiding Your Rocks	60
Finding Other Rocks	62
Tracking Your Rock Finds	64
Throwing a Rock Painting Party	66
Hidden Rocks Log	68
Found Rocks Log	74

Welcome to the Wonderful World of...

PAINTING ROCKS

It's the latest rockin' craze!

Rock painting is all about:
- getting creative and decorating stones
- hiding them in public places for others to find
- searching outdoors for other painted rocks to keep or pass on to others
- connecting with a huge social media community to share finds and designs
- brightening someone's day!

Anything goes for the designs – get inspirational with uplifting words or pictures, let out your artistic side with pretty patterns or cute animals, or just go crazy with monsters and munchies. Try out the designs suggested in this book and then come up with your own, too!

No matter what you paint, it's all about joining in and putting a smile on someone's face when they come across your stone in the wild.

Go ahead... rock on!

You will need:

Rocks
Although you can find rocks almost everywhere, you can't take them from just anywhere. DON'T help yourself to stones from beaches, national parks, memorials or businesses. Instead, find them in your garden, or buy big packs at supermarkets or homeware shops. Bags of cobblestones give a great selection of shapes and sizes for your designs.

Paint
All sorts of paint works for this - use what you already have at home if you can! Acrylic paints work best of all and you can find these at craft or bargain shops.

Pens
For finer details or drawings, colourful permanent markers work really well. These are also ideal for writing the details of your online group on the base of the rock.

Sealant
It's important to seal your rock to keep your design safe in the wild. Outdoor varnish or spray sealant works best for this. Find it at craft or homeware shops. Ask a grown-up for help buying and using this.

Other bits and bobs
paintbrushes: gather together a selection of big and small ones

water: for cleaning paintbrushes after using different colours

kitchen roll: for drying the brushes and wiping the ends

paper plates: to use as a paint palette

surface covers, such as newspaper, plastic sheets and aprons: to protect your work surfaces and clothes

Getting Started

Choosing the perfect rocks

You can turn most rocks into masterpieces, but some rocks are easier to use than others:

- Look for smooth stones
- Consider the shape of the rocks for your design
- Think about how dark or light your rocks are. Dark-coloured rocks work well for white or metallic pen designs. Light-coloured stones are great for designs that are drawn on with pens.

Prepping your rocks

Before you do any painting, wash your rocks with washing-up liquid and warm water, rinse well, then let them dry. Lay them in the sun to help them dry quicker.

TIP: If your rocks have any rough spots on them, you can use sandpaper to smooth them out.

Prepping your design

Look online, around you and through this book for ideas. Once you know what you're going to draw, practise on a piece of paper first. When you're ready to move on to the rocks, you can use a pencil to draw the designs on before painting, if needed.

Passing it on

Look online to find your local Facebook rock painting group. Try searching on Facebook for the name of your town + 'painting rocks'. If this doesn't work, try the nearest big city, your region or even your country instead. These groups give you loads of ideas for designs, as well as where to hide and find rocks. Make sure you write the group name on the back of your rocks, with a message to the lucky people who find them, such as: 'Post a pic to [insert the name of your Facebook rock group here] and re-hide.' This way you should see posts pop up when your pebbles are discovered.

Finishing up

Once you're happy with your designs, ask a grown-up to help you to seal the rocks with varnish or spray to set your art in stone. Then go out and find the perfect hiding places!

Tips and Tricks

Paint the biggest sections of your design first and the smallest sections last.

Be patient! Allow the paint to dry between coats and colours to avoid any smudging. You can ask an adult to help you use a hairdryer if you want to make the paint dry quicker.

Painting a white base coat on a dark stone helps the colours to stand out better. Apply two coats and let these dry thoroughly before starting your design.

The number of coats of paint you'll need depends on the darkness of the rock and the lightness of the paint. Use your judgement and stop when you feel the paint is solid enough.

When you're painting the whole rock one colour, start with the sides so you can place your finger in the middle of the rock to keep it steady. Then lay the rock on your covered work surface so you can fill in any gaps (e.g. where your finger was!).

Use wide paintbrushes for painting big sections and small brushes or fine pens for details.

DESIGN
Cute Creatures

Create all sorts of adorable animals to hide outside. Just imagine a stone bug peeking out of the grass at the park or a penguin pebble perching on a tree stump! Work with the shape of the rock to make your stone into the animal itself or draw creature portraits in the middle of the rock.

Little Ladybird

1. Using red paint, cover the top and sides of a round stone. Use sweeping motions around the sides for a smoother look. Leave to dry. Apply another coat (or more) if needed, depending on the darkness of your rock. Leave to dry.

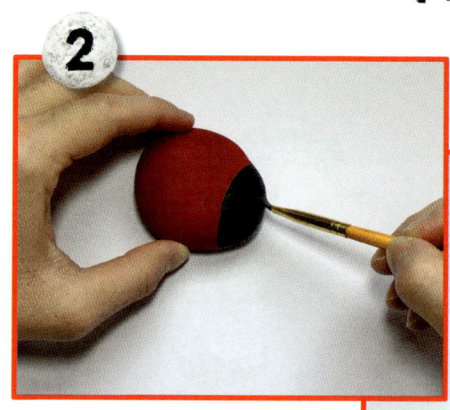

2. Paint a rounded black shape on one end of the rock for the face.

3. Paint a black line down the centre of the rock.

Dip the handle of a thin paintbrush into black paint. Dot it gently on the ladybird's back to create the dots.

Use the handle of a thin, clean paintbrush to create two white paint dots for eyes. Leave to dry.

Dip a pencil tip into black paint. Dot it gently inside each white eye to create a small black pupil. You can also use a cocktail stick or the end of a paintbrush, depending on how big you want the pupils. Leave to dry.

TIP:
Wipe the paint off your pencil with kitchen roll as soon as you've finished the dots so it doesn't dry on there!

On the bottom of the rock, use a fine permanent marker to write your message. This could be something like: 'Post a pic to [your Facebook rock group] and re-hide.'
Ask a grown-up to help you to seal your rock using varnish or spray in a safe open space.

Hide your rock in a public place!

13

Bee

Add to your rock insects with this happy little bee. Paint a rock yellow then add stripes, wings, eyes and a little smile. You may need several coats of yellow paint to cover a darker rock. **Buzz buzz!**

Snail

Make a taller rock into a super-cute snail. Choose a fun colour for the shell then add a friendly face and antennae with fine paintbrushes or pens. Don't forget the trademark shell spiral!

Hedgehog

This sleepy stone needs just light brown, dark brown and black paint. Choose a rock with a slightly pointed end if possible, for the hedgehog's nose. Add as many spikes as you like!

Fish

Use a light-coloured flat rock as an underwater canvas for a fun fish. Try using your permanent markers instead of paints for a finer design.

Penguin

A large triangular rock makes a pebble-tastic penguin! Draw your design on the rock in pencil first to get the shape of the body and wings right. Paint the white section (a couple of coats if necessary), allow to dry, and then add the black paint for the body and details.

DESIGN

Words of Wisdom

The painted rock trend started as a way to pass on kindness to a total stranger. Go back to basics with positive words of wisdom to make someone smile.

Use paint or pens in whatever colour you like to write messages on your rocks. Try out different types of lettering for different effects.

Check out pages 56-59 for inspiration for more words of wisdom or come up with your own!

YOU GOT THIS

You rock!

HIDING HINT: Think about your messages and who they'd help. For example, hide 'good luck' stones near a school at exam time or a 'listen to your mum' rock in town around Mother's Day.

BE YOU!

Psst! You're amazing. Pass it on!

Step it up a notch with little pictures and patterns to go with your words. It's a double whammy of positive energy for whoever finds your rock!

TIP: Try metallic permanent markers for a shiny effect.

18

TIP:
Paint the rock and then use pens to create a dainty frame for your words.

DESIGN

Inspiring Images

Take the idea of spreading smiles, love and sunshine literally with pretty pictures that show these very things. A dainty heart, sunny sun, uplifting rainbow and smiley stone are sure to brighten the day of the person who finds it. Inspire away!

Dainty Dotty Heart

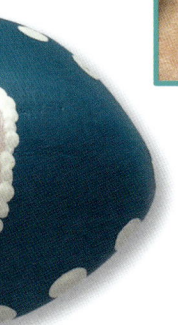

Paint the top of an oval-shaped stone a nice bright colour. Leave to dry. Apply another coat (or more) if needed. Leave to dry.

Draw a heart shape in the centre of the rock in pencil.

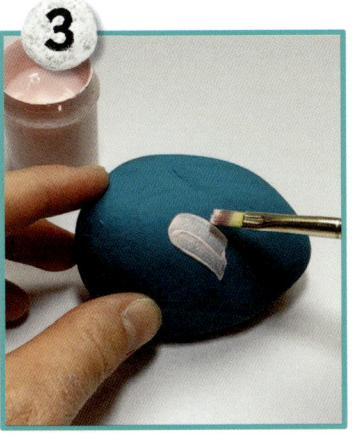

Using a small paintbrush, fill in the heart shape with light pink paint. Leave to dry. Apply a second coat and allow to dry again.

Using the handle of a fine paintbrush, apply small dots around the edge of the heart.

Using the handle of a larger paintbrush, draw large dots spaced evenly apart around the edge of the background oval. Leave it to dry.

On the bottom of the rock, use a fine permanent marker to write your message. This could be something like: 'Post a pic to [your Facebook rock group] and re-hide.'
Ask a grown-up to help you to seal your rock using varnish or spray in a safe open space.

Hide your rock in a public place!

Flowers

Make smiles blossom by planting rock flowers around town. For a delicate daisy, paint sweeping white strokes outwards from a yellow centre. Allow to dry and then add darker yellow dots to the yellow circle with the handle of a paintbrush to create a raised effect. Or, go for a less-is-more approach with a simple flower in friendly bright colours.

HIDING HINT: Have fun tucking these stones in places as bright as they are. Hide flower pebbles amongst wild flowers and place your sun pebble on a sandy beach for a truly tropical find.

Sun

There's no better way to brighten a day than by bringing out the sun. Start by drawing the sun with rays on your rock in pencil. Then paint the blue background and leave to dry. Lastly, paint the yellow areas, using a base coat of white if needed.

Rainbow

Somewhere over the rainbow... there's a rock waiting to be found. Paint one colour at a time and let the paint dry after each colour to avoid smudging.

Smiley Face

The ultimate way to pass on a grin! Paint a solid yellow circle (using at least two coats) and allow to dry. Use the back of a thin paintbrush for dots for the eyes and then add the all-important smile.

There are loads of other inspirational images you could paint. How about a butterfly or even a unicorn? Have a look at pages 52-55 for more inspiring ideas.

DESIGN
Cool Colours

A super-simple but super-effective rock design, coloured stones are a guaranteed way to add some colour to someone's day.

Simply Red Rock

1. Paint the rock's top and sides one solid colour. Use at least two coats for a good coverage, and more if needed for lighter colours such as yellow and orange. Leave to dry.

2. Write the colour on the top or side of the rock using black paint or a pen.

3. On the bottom of the rock, use a fine permanent marker to write your message. This could be something like 'Post a pic to [your Facebook rock group] and re-hide.' **Ask a grown-up to help you to seal your rock using varnish or spray in a safe open space.**

HIDING HINT: Post your rainbow of rocks to Facebook and see if people in the group can find them all!

TIP: Choose lighter rocks for the lighter colours or use a base coat of white first.

Repeat for as many colours as you have paint and stones!

TIP: Instead of black, you could use paint or a pen in the colour of the rock (e.g. write 'red' in red ink on the red background). Just test first to be sure the word will show up!

Shades

Paint blocky shapes using shades of the same main colour, such as light, bright and dark blue. Label with the colour's name as before.

Frames

Paint the rock in a single solid colour. Then use a permanent marker in the same colour to draw a fun frame for the word.

Dots

Instead of painting the whole rock in the featured colour, go for a minimal look with just one sophisticated spot in the centre.

Metallics

Scribble on a dark rock with a metallic pen to create a truly amazing treasure. Try gold, silver or bronze for what will feel like a real gem to find!

DESIGN
Pretty Patterns

Patterned pebbles can be as simple or as detailed as you like – either way, they're sure to be eye-catching! Try a modern version of a mandala (a symbol of universal balance); create cool, contemporary shapes, or just go for striking spots and stripes.

Modern Mandala

1. In the centre of a round rock, draw a circle in pencil. Fill it in with black paint. Leave to dry.

2. In the centre of the black circle, use a small paintbrush to paint a small white circle.

Using the tip of a pencil, paint bright pink dots around the white centre. Start with dots in the 12, 3, 6 and 9 o'clock positions, and then fill in the gaps for equal spacing.

Using the handle of a medium-sized paintbrush, make bright pink dots around the small dots.

TIP: You don't have to use the colours suggested here. Use whatever paints you've got and whatever colours you fancy!

Using the handle of a large paintbrush, add slightly bigger dots in purple paint. Space each one between the pink dots, as shown.

Using the handle of the paintbrush, draw even bigger dots in bright green paint. Space these between the purple dots, overlapping the edges of your black circle. Leave all dots to dry.

Continued on next page...

Using a straightened paper clip or a cocktail stick, make tiny white dots in the centre of the larger pink and purple dots.

Using a pencil, dot white paint around each green dot, as shown. To keep the balance, make the same number of dots around each one. Leave to dry.

On the bottom of the rock, use a fine permanent marker to write your message. This could be something like 'Post a pic to [your Facebook rock group] and re-hide.'
Ask a grown-up to help you to seal your rock using varnish or spray in a safe open space.

Hide your rock in a public place!

Geometric Shapes

Use angular shapes for a trendy triangular look. Paint your stone white and then paint different-shaped triangles in two funky colours. Once dry, use a black permanent marker to draw the same triangle shapes over the top, slightly offset from the painted ones.

Simple Spots and Stripes

You can't go wrong with classic spots and stripes! Start with a white base coat then add stripes or spots in whatever pattern you can think of.

DESIGN

Fun Food

These scrumptious stones are *almost* good enough to eat! Paint fun fruit, tempting treats and even funny faces for the cutest little (pretend) nibbles to pick up in the wild.

Sweet Strawberry

1. Paint a triangular stone red. Use two coats if necessary. Leave to dry.

2. Paint a green leaf shape at the top of the strawberry, on the flat end.

Using a fine paintbrush, add little brown seeds. Leave to dry.

On the back of the rock, use a fine permanent marker to write your message. This could be something like 'Post a pic to [your Facebook rock group] and re-hide.'
Ask a grown-up to help you to seal your rock using varnish or spray in a safe open space.

Hide your rock in a public place!

Watermelon

Run wild with the fruit theme and paint a juicy watermelon on another triangular stone. Start by painting the stone red, then add a light green strip and a dark green strip at the bottom. Do one colour straight after the other (no need to wait for the paint to dry) so the edges blend together slightly. Leave all this to dry then paint on brown seeds.

HIDING HINT: Hide these underneath picnic tables or even near supermarkets for some foodie fun!

Doughnut

For the stone seeker with a sweet tooth, try a delicious donut! Start with a light brown base coat, then add a thick ring of icing. Once this is dry, use dark brown to define the icing and the hole in the centre. Then add sprinkles!

Pizza

Pizza-rrific! Pebble-tastic! Start with a light brown base coat on a flat round stone. Once dry, paint some yellow cheese. Let that dry, then use brown paint to define the crust. Finally, add your toppings!

Faces

For extra food fun, draw or paint faces on them, for fruit that is too cute!

DESIGN
Black and White

There's a lot you can do with just two colours. Play with white on black and black on white for some seriously stand-out stones.

smile often

HIDING HINT: These arty stones would be very much at home hidden outside art galleries, museums or by statues.

BE YOU!

White on Black

Start with a dark-coloured stone or paint your stone black. Once it's dry, use only white paint for your design. Try leaves, flowers, patterns and even simple scenes that will stand out on the black background.

Constellations

A stone that has been painted black is the perfect base for a starry night. Add dots with white paint and join them up to create a constellation. Try the big dipper or paint your star sign to make it personal!

Yin and Yang

Go for both white on black and black on white to create this Chinese symbol of contrasting yet complementary forces.

Panda

Start with a couple of white base coats, then use black paint for the ears, eyes, nose and mouth of this cute creature. Once dry, use a pencil for the white eye dots. Finally, once that's dry, use a cocktail stick or straightened paper clip for the tiny black pupils.

Silhouettes

Go a step further and create cool black silhouettes on a background colour other than white. Try drawing a simple black tree shape in permanent marker on a lilac base or go for a dark pink evening sky, complete with a white full moon and a silhouetted owl on a branch drawn or painted in black.

DESIGN
Location, Location

Leave a memento of where you're from for someone else to find. This could be a flag, your favourite landmark or a special setting. Hide the stone locally or leave it somewhere when you're on holiday so whoever finds it can see a little bit of your hometown. Travel the world!

Union Flag

Draw your flag's details in pencil.

For the Union Flag, use a small paintbrush to paint the central red cross. Leave to dry.
Then use another small paintbrush to paint the white borders and diagonals, as shown. Leave to dry.

TIP: Look up a picture of the flag online for reference.

SAFETY WARNING
Never give out your home address or personal details.

Use a fine paintbrush to paint a red stripe in each of the white diagonals.

Carefully, use a fine paintbrush to paint the remaining sections blue. Leave to dry.

On the bottom of the rock, use a fine permanent marker to write your message. This could be something like 'Post a pic to [your Facebook rock group] and re-hide.'
Ask a grown-up to help you to seal your rock using varnish or spray in a safe open space.

Hide your rock in a public place!

Setting

Choose something that shows off your part of the world. Maybe you live by the seaside, near hills or in the city. Or perhaps there's a specific tree or bridge that's special to your area. What represents home?

Home Sweet Home

Create dreamy rocks with pretty pictures of your dream home. Paint a base colour then use fine permanent markers for the details.

Snapshot

For a picture-perfect pebble, try a clever mobile phone design to showcase taking a photo of a favourite spot.

Landmark

Instead of showing off your own location, choose a favourite famous landmark. How about the Statue of Liberty, the Taj Mahal or this Eiffel Tower drawn in metallic pens on a dark painted background? **Fantastique!**

DESIGN
Little Monsters

Give someone a friendly fright with these cheeky little monsters! Have fun drawing all sorts of different faces and make a whole monster family to hide out in the wild.

Big Nose

1. Paint a tall stone bright green. Use two coats if necessary. Allow to dry.

2. Using a small paintbrush, paint a dark green oval nose. Leave to dry.

3. Using the handle of a small paintbrush, draw two white eyes. Allow to dry.

4

Using a black permanent marker, draw an outline around the eyes and nose. Add pupils in the eyes and draw a smile with teeth.

5

Using the tip of a pencil, carefully fill in the teeth with white paint. Leave to dry.

6

On the base of the rock, use a fine permanent marker to write your message. This could be something like 'Post a pic to [your Facebook rock group] and re-hide'.

Ask a grown-up to help you to seal your rock using varnish or spray in a safe open space.

7 Hide your rock in a public place!

HIDING HINT:
Hide these little friends along neighbourhood streets at Halloween. Or, if you can't wait until then, place them outside a seaside cave for a little bit of monster mischief. Boo!

Always check the tide and take an adult with you.

Funny Faces

Multiplying monsters! Paint more rocks in beastly bright colours and then draw a different face on each one. Try out grins and frowns, no teeth or lots of teeth, rounded or triangular eyes. This is your chance to go wild!

Happy Families

Make a happy little family of monsters and hide all of them together for a MONSTROUSLY good find!

DESIGN
Shaped Rocks

Instead of deciding on a design you want to paint first, be inspired by the shape of your stones. Look closely at your rocks... What do you see? Here are some examples, but go with wherever your own shaped stones take you!

before

before

Bird

Shark

Houses

Tall or triangular rocks make perfect houses. Imagine your dream home or go for a simple abstract look.

Cars

Use felt-tip pens to draw detailed cars on vehicle-shaped rocks. Don't forget to add passengers!

More Sea Creatures

So many rocks want to be fish, sharks and sea monsters. Look at the shape of the rocks you've got and see what ideas swim to mind.

People

Use round and oval pebbles to create rockin' models of your family and friends. Have fun with hairstyles and clothes to represent each person. Which stone will you be?

Art Templates

For a bit of artistic help, try copying these pictures onto your stones. Or just use them as inspiration!

More Art Templates

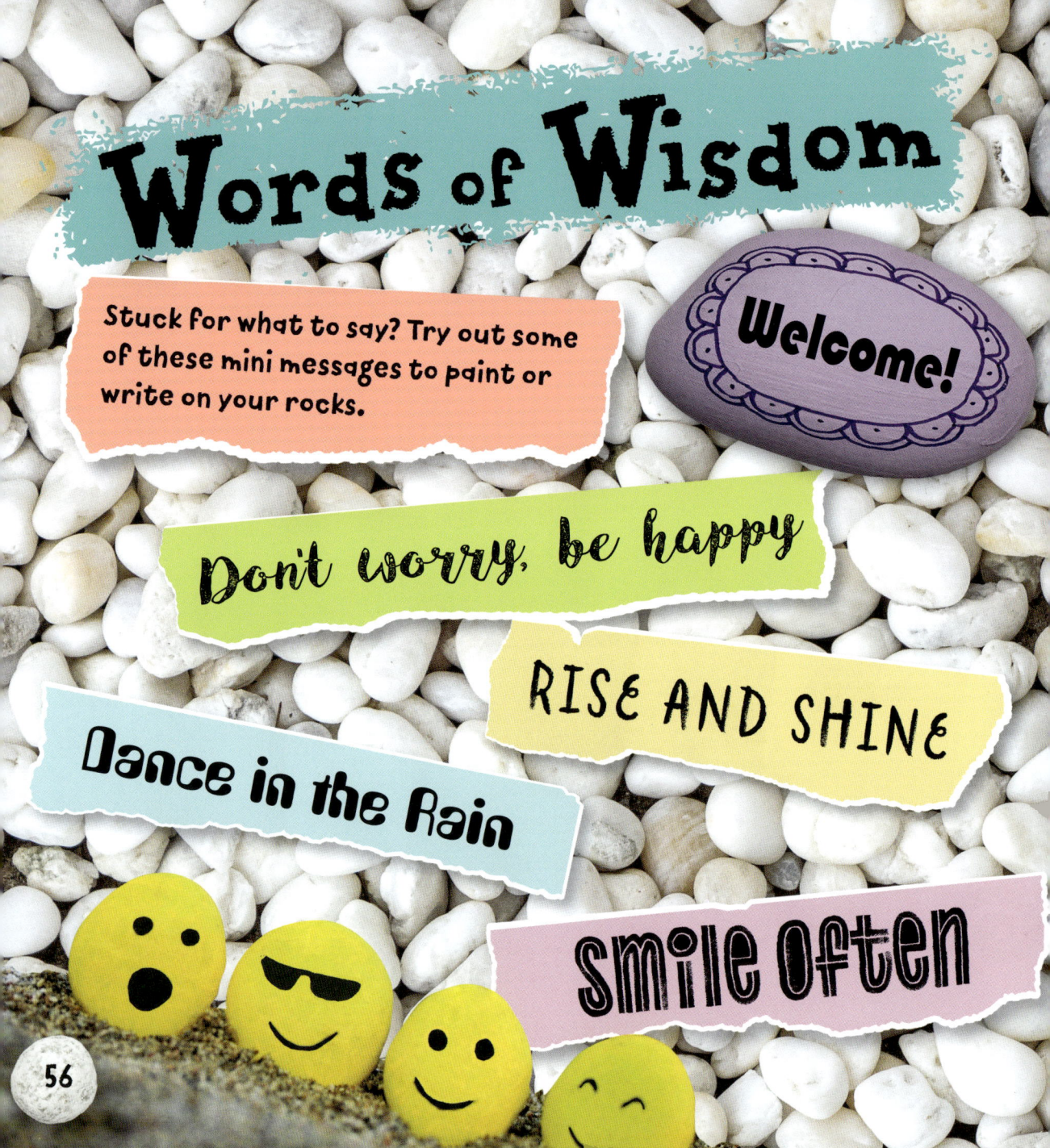

Words of Wisdom

Stuck for what to say? Try out some of these mini messages to paint or write on your rocks.

Welcome!

Don't worry, be happy

RISE AND SHINE

Dance in the Rain

Smile Often

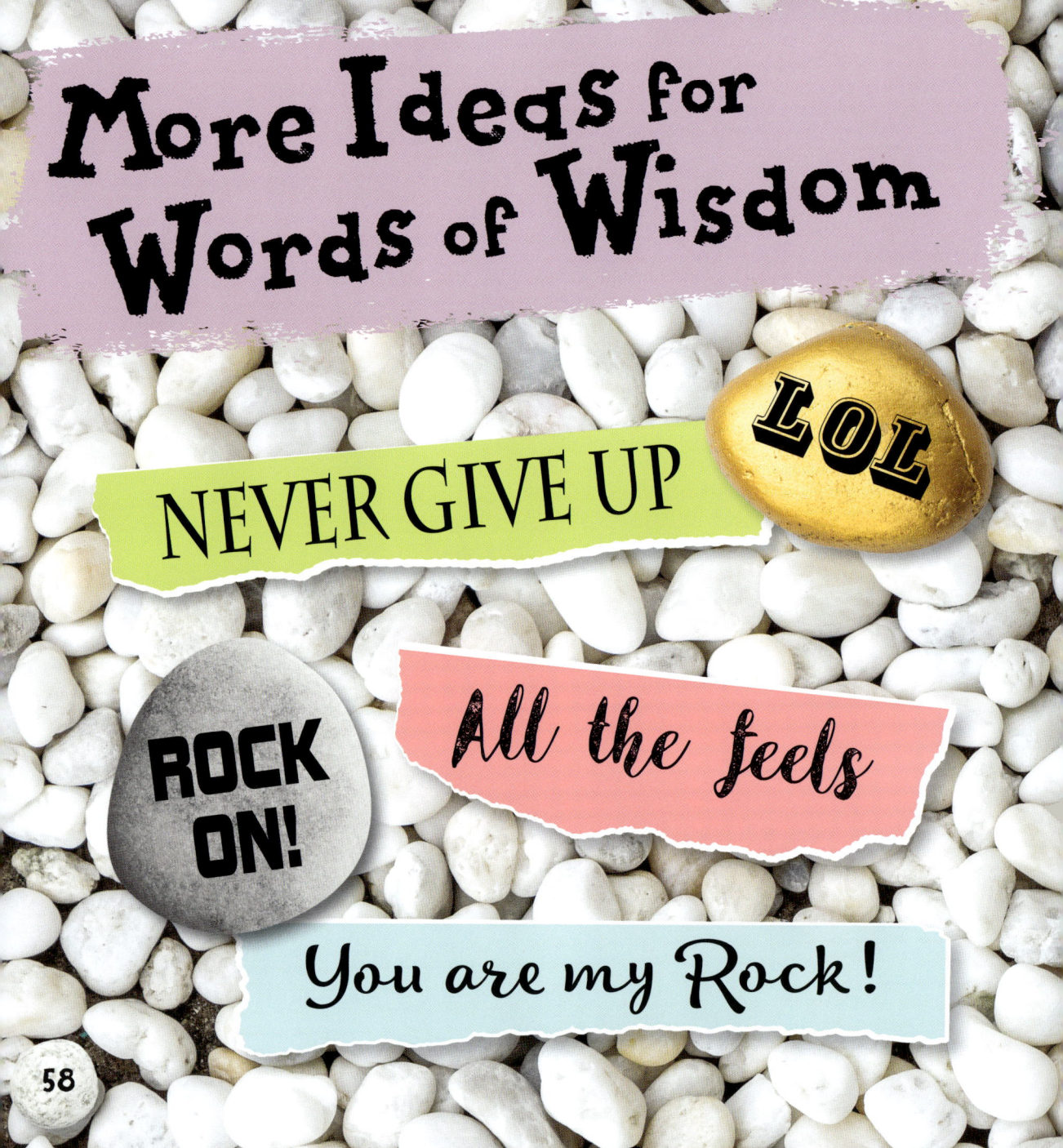

Hiding Your Rocks

Once you've painted your pebbles, or come across rocks in the wild, you'll be itching to share them! Here are some handy dos and don'ts to keep in mind when you go hiding:

 **DO** hide rocks in public places, such as parks, walking trails and around town.

 **Don't** hide rocks on private property (unless it's your own garden for a fun game with family and friends!).

 **DO** think about places where the rocks are partly hidden but can be discovered in a fun way, such as peeking out from a bush or sitting on a bench.

 **DO** be safe! DON'T hide rocks where people can trip over them or where they could fall down on top of people.

 consider hiding rocks on your friends' front doorsteps to get them involved.

 join a Facebook rock group and look there for ideas of good hiding places.

 go out alone or after dark.

 post clues in the Facebook rock group to lead people to your rocks.

 always take an adult with you and stay in well-lit, public spaces.

 forget to label the back of your rock with the Facebook rock group so that you'll be able to see when your rock has been discovered.

 DON'T be disappointed if your rock never shows up in the Facebook group. Some people don't have Facebook or can't post for whatever reason, but you can still be sure the rock will brighten someone's day and is enjoying its travels.

Finding other Rocks

Painting and hiding rocks is only half the fun – the other half is all about going out on adventures to find little stone surprises of your own!

Here are some top tips for finding rocks:

Have a look on your local Facebook rock page for clues of where rocks are hidden.

Check where other people in the rock group have found rocks – this gives you an idea of good places to look.

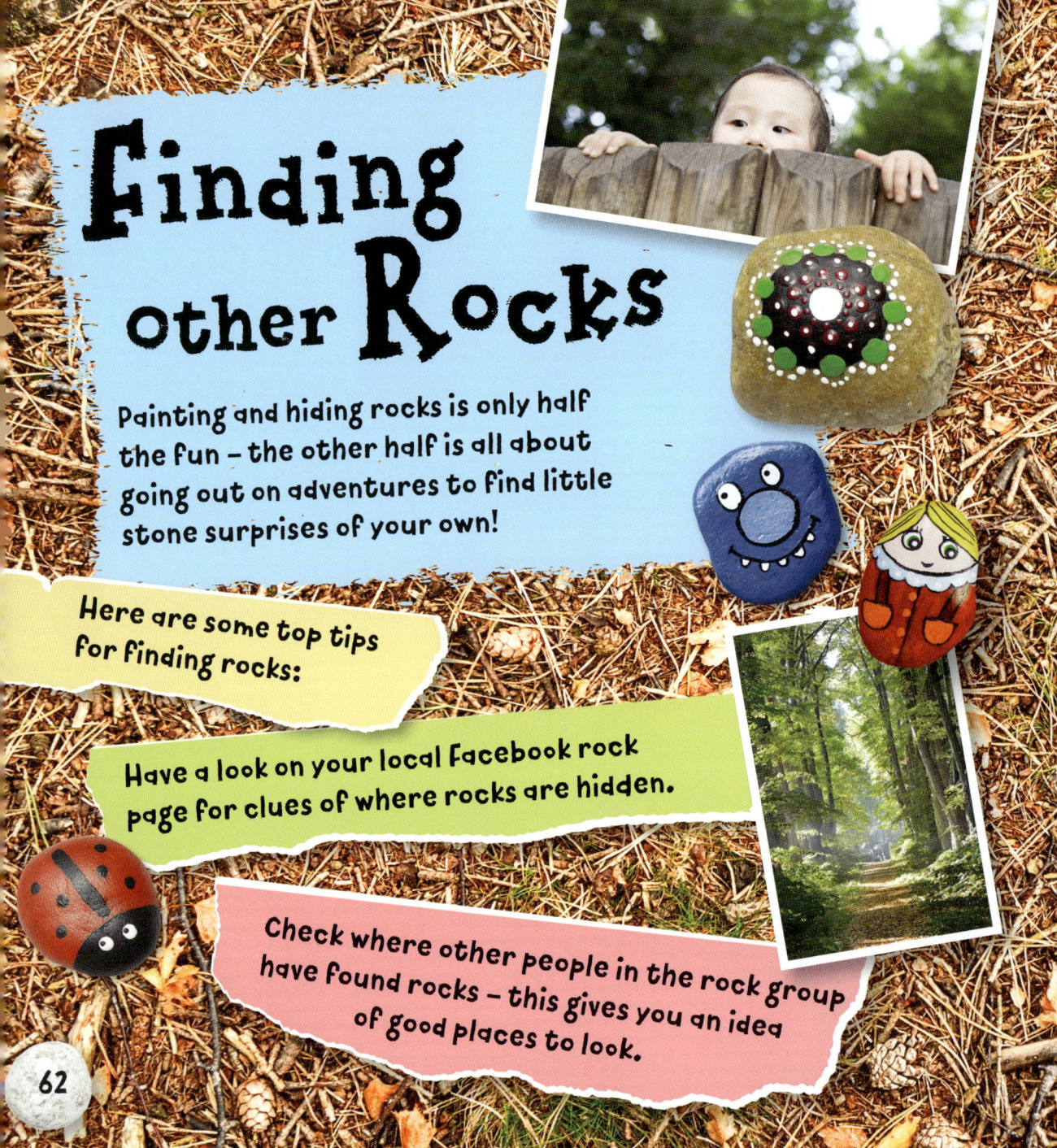

Look up and down and all around in public places such as parks and walking trails.

Keep your eyes peeled on major routes, such as when walking to school or on the high street.

Play a game of rocks hide-and-seek with friends by hiding rocks for each other in a designated space such as a park, where you can guarantee success.

And finally... don't look too hard. You never know when you might just come across a sneaky little stone!

63

Tracking Your Rock Finds

So you've found a rock – congratulations! Now what?

1 Check the rock for the Facebook group information.

2 Take a picture of the rock.

3 Post the picture and details about where you found it to the Facebook group. Someone out there is waiting to know if their rock has been found and your post will brighten their day!

4 Re-hide the rock to spread the smiles or keep it as a souvenir if it's just too nice to part with.

5 Write down the details of your discovery in the log at the back of this book. How many rocks can you find?

ROCK DESCRIPTION	DRAWING OF ROCK	WHERE IT WAS FOUND	DATE FOUND	POSTED TO FACEBOOK?	WHERE (IF) RE-HIDDEN	DATE RE-HIDDEN	POSTED TO FACEBOOK?
Blue heart rock		Forest Park	15 July	YES - Forest Park group	In a tree	18 July	YES - photo and clue given
Sun rock		Sandy Beach	23 July	YES - Beach Bay group	Kept it at home	N/A	YES
Yellow smiley face rock		High Street	30 July	YES - Blueville Town group	On the café steps	31 July	YES - photo and clue given
Blue monster face rock							

Throwing a Rock Painting Party

Rock painting doesn't have to be a solo activity... throw a pebble-tastic party to get friends and family involved, too. Here are some tips on how to host a party that ROCKS:

The prep
Gather together enough supplies (rocks, paints, paintbrushes, water, paper plates, kitchen roll, etc.) for everyone. Cover all your work surfaces with plenty of newspaper so you don't have to worry about mess and to make the clean-up easier for yourself later.

The party
Rock painting in a group is an event in itself, but you can add to the party feel with snack food and rockin' music.

The big night

Some of your guests might not know about rock painting, so your first task will be filling them in on what it's all about. You might want to have some art templates or words of wisdom as inspiration for those who are nervous about their artistic abilities. KEEP THIS BOOK AT THE READY!

The painting

Your guests might just want to do their own thing, but it can also be really fun to choose a theme for the painting party — for example, everyone could paint their own rock monster or you could go with an animal theme and come up with a whole zoo of rock animals by the end of the night. Or, try tag-team painting: paint part of a rock and then pass it on to the next person to add more details.

The after-party

You may need to seal all the rocks yourself if the paint isn't dry when people are ready to leave. Remember to get an adult to help you. This gives you an excuse to gather everyone together again for them to collect their rocks. Turn this into a second party, where everyone goes out together to hide their artwork and guess who might be the first to find a rock while you're out, too!

Hidden Rocks Log

Keep track of all your gorgeous creations with drawings and notes in this log before you hide the stones to pass on to others. See how many rocks have been reported found!

ROCK DESCRIPTION	DRAWING OF ROCK	WHERE IT WAS HIDDEN	DATE HIDDEN	POSTED TO FACEBOOK?	REPORTED FOUND ON FACEBOOK?	DATE REPORTED FOUND
eg. Ladybird		Mountain Park	20 June	YES - photo and clue given	YES!	30 June

ROCK DESCRIPTION	DRAWING OF ROCK	WHERE IT WAS HIDDEN	DATE HIDDEN	POSTED TO FACEBOOK?	REPORTED FOUND ON FACEBOOK?	DATE REPORTED FOUND

ROCK DESCRIPTION	DRAWING OF ROCK	WHERE IT WAS HIDDEN	DATE HIDDEN	POSTED TO FACEBOOK?	REPORTED FOUND ON FACEBOOK?	DATE REPORTED FOUND

Rock Description	Drawing of Rock	Where it was Hidden	Date Hidden	Posted to Facebook?	Reported Found on Facebook?	Date Reported Found

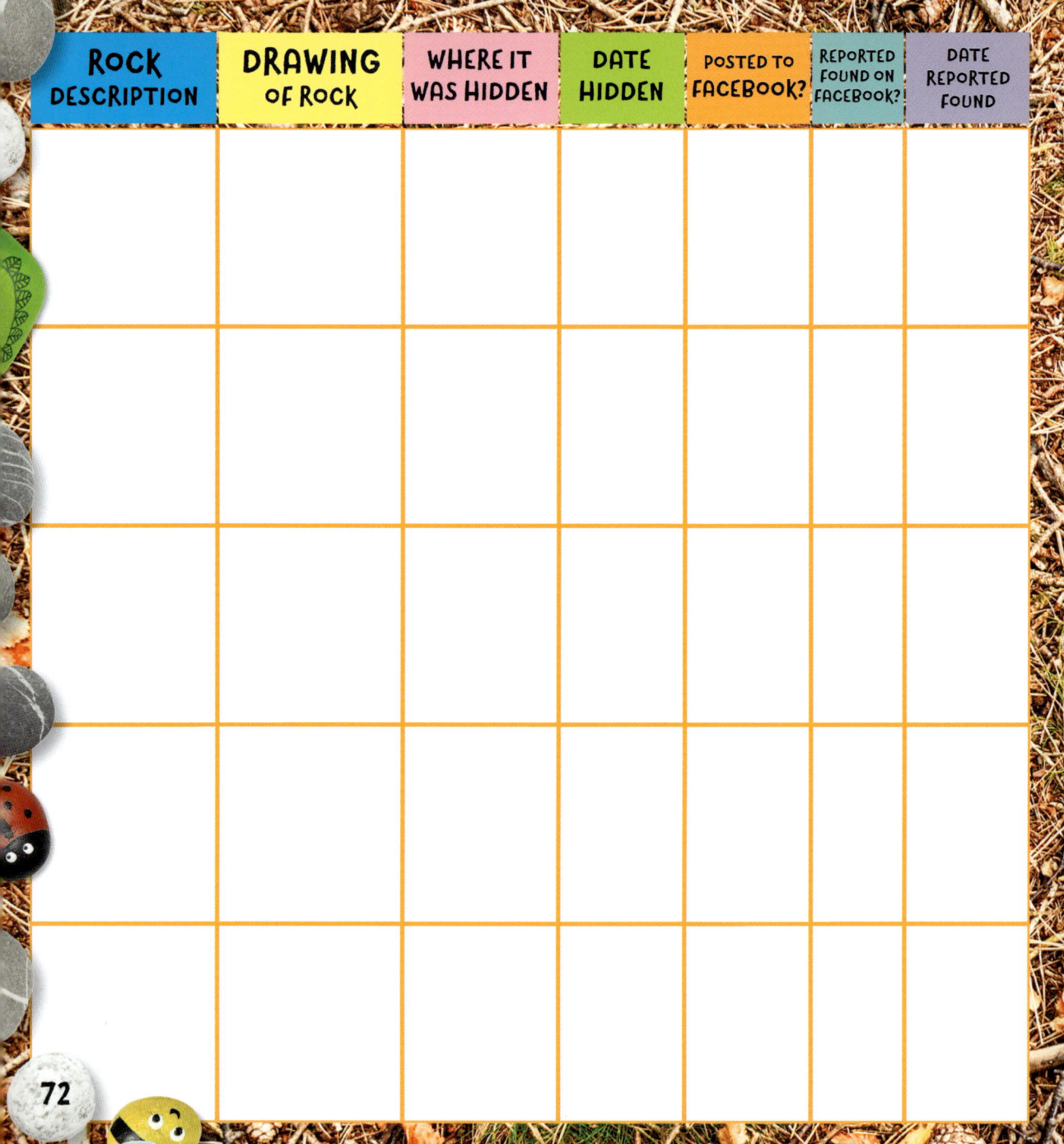

Rock Description	Drawing of Rock	Where It Was Hidden	Date Hidden	Posted to Facebook?	Reported Found on Facebook?	Date Reported Found

Found Rocks Log

Don't forget to log all of your rockin' finds, too! How many painted rocks can you discover in the wild? Which is your favourite?

ROCK DESCRIPTION	DRAWING OF ROCK	WHERE IT WAS FOUND	DATE FOUND	POSTED TO FACEBOOK?	WHERE (IF) RE-HIDDEN	DATE RE-HIDDEN	POSTED TO FACEBOOK?
eg. Blue heart rock	💙	Forest Park	15 July	YES - Forest Park group	In a tree	18 July	YES - photo and clue given

ROCK DESCRIPTION	DRAWING OF ROCK	WHERE IT WAS FOUND	DATE FOUND	POSTED TO FACEBOOK?	WHERE (IF) RE-HIDDEN	DATE RE-HIDDEN	POSTED TO FACEBOOK?

Rock Description	Drawing of Rock	Where it was Found	Date Found	Posted to Facebook?	Where (if) Re-Hidden	Date Re-Hidden	Posted to Facebook?

ROCK DESCRIPTION	DRAWING OF ROCK	WHERE IT WAS FOUND	DATE FOUND	POSTED TO FACEBOOK?	WHERE (IF) RE-HIDDEN	DATE RE-HIDDEN	POSTED TO FACEBOOK?

ROCK DESCRIPTION	DRAWING OF ROCK	WHERE IT WAS FOUND	DATE FOUND	POSTED TO FACEBOOK?	WHERE (IF) RE-HIDDEN	DATE RE-HIDDEN	POSTED TO FACEBOOK?

Rock Description	Drawing of Rock	Where it was Found	Date Found	Posted to Facebook?	Where (if) Re-Hidden	Date Re-Hidden	Posted to Facebook?

Credits

Ekatarina_Minaeva / Shutterstock.com: p1, 23, 59; photokup / Shutterstock.com: p2, 14-15, 50-51, 74-79; Big Foot Productions / Shutterstock.com: p2, 6-7, 8-80; kbecca / Shutterstock.com: all pages; Ekatarina_Minaeva / Shutterstock.com: p3; Tamara Kulikova / Shutterstock.com: p3, 37; Cagkan Sayin / Shutterstock.com: p3, 31, 52; Felix Furo / Shutterstock.com: p3; Myimages - Micha / Shutterstock.com: p3; Africa Studio / Shutterstock.com: p4-5, 7, 12-13, 16-17, 20-21, 24-25, p28, 30, 32-33, 44-45, 49; Satori Studio / Shutterstock.com: p3, 13, 16-17, 20-21, 25, 29, 32-33, 48, 65; Vakidzasi / Shutterstock.com: p4, 11, 51, 62; FabrikaSimf / Shutterstock.com: p7, 12-13, 16-17, 20-21, 24-25, 28-29, 32-33. 44-45, 48-49; schab / Shutterstock.com: p8; JungleOutThere / Shutterstock.com: p9, 53; chelovector / Shutterstock.com: p9, 52; bergia / Shutterstock.com: p9, 57; Northern-Light / Shutterstock.com: p8-9, 22-23, 62-63, 68-73; AVS-Images / Shutterstock.com: p10-11, 16-17, 56-57, 58-59, 62-63, 64-65; Edda Dupree / Shutterstock.com: p10-11, 46-47, shambhavi pandey / Shutterstock.com: p11, 36-37; Twisted Pixels / Shutterstock.com: p13; perlphoto / Shutterstock.com: p21; Ekatarina_Minaeva / Shutterstock.com: p22; Kamenetskly Konstantin / Shutterstock.com: p30; Yuliia Yakovyna / Shutterstock.com: p31; MR BUDDEE WIANGNGORN / Shutterstock.com: p31, 42-43; Valentina Razumova / Shutterstock.com: p33; vulcano / Shutterstock.com: p34-35; Andrey_Kuzmin / Shutterstock.com: p34-35; Guiyuan Chen / Shutterstock.com: p34-35; Nadya_Art / Shutterstock.com: p35; Zhe Vasylieva / Shutterstock.com: p35; n_defender / Shutterstock.com: p36, 43, 45; Tamara Kulikova / Shutterstock.com: p37; Tamara Kulikova / Shutterstock.com: p37; VectorHappy / Shutterstock.com: p37; Vitalii Gaidukov / Shutterstock.com: p38; D_D / Shutterstock.com: p38-39; yournameonstones / Shutterstock.com: p40, 43; nito / Shutterstock.com: p41; Myimages - Micha / Shutterstock.com: p40-41; SLdesign / Shutterstock.com: p41; Khmelnitskaia Evgeniia / Shutterstock.com: p42; Benvenuto Cellini / Shutterstock.com: p42; Shaun Jeffers / Shutterstock.com: p45; Tatiana Ermakova / Shutterstock.com: p46-47, 66-67; Jelena Yukka / Shutterstock.com: p47; str0pe / Shutterstock.com: p47, 67; Raffaellla Galvani / Shutterstock.com: p50; snova / Shutterstock.com: p50; bergia / Shutterstock.com: p50, 51; daisybee / Shutterstock.com: p52-53; danjazzia / Shutterstock.com: p52; Little Apple / Shutterstock.com: p52-53; Pravokrugulnik / Shutterstock.com: p52; ExpressVectors / Shutterstock.com: p52-53; Geometric Complexity / Shutterstock.com: p53; picnote / Shutterstock.com: p53; Sudowoodo / Shutterstock.com: p53; twobears_ art / Shutterstock.com: p53-54; Elina Li / Shutterstock.com: p54; davorana / Shutterstock.com: p54; SoleilC / Shutterstock.com: p54; Vector Bakery / Shutterstock.com: p55; La Gorda / Shutterstock.com: p55; Pravokrugulnik / Shutterstock.com: p55; Supza / Shutterstock.com: p55; NotionPic / Shutterstock.com: p55; indiovetorepurodotcom / Shutterstock.com: p55; Sathaphorn Suriyon / Shutterstock.com: p56-59; Steve Parsley / Shutterstock.com: p56; Purino / Shutterstock.com: p62; Aleksey Stemmer / Shutterstock.com: p62; sevenke / Shutterstock.com: p63; Karin Bredenberg / Shutterstock.com: p63; Tom Gowanlock / Shutterstock.com: p63; Diego Cervo / Shutterstock.com: p63; Dmitri Ma / Shutterstock.com: p64; wavebreakmedia / Shutterstock.com: p64; Luba Shushpanova / Shutterstock.com: p66; Ramona Kaulitzki / Shutterstock.com: p66; AnastasiaKopa / Shutterstock.com: p66; MNStudio / Shutterstock.com: p67; LegART / Shutterstock.com: p80.